THE BEST 50

CHICKEN BREAST RECIPES

Joanna White

BRISTOL PUBLISHING ENTERPRISES
San Leandro, California

Printed in the United States of America.

ISBN 1-55867-125-0

Cover design: Paredes Design Associates
Cover photography: John A. Benson
Food stylist: Suzanne Carreiro

BUYING, STORING AND COOKING CHICKEN

Chicken lends itself readily to variation because it is mild-flavored and is compatible with almost every vegetable, herb and spice. It is a lean, low-cholesterol meat that is ideal for our health-conscious society. Almost every country in the world has chicken in its cuisine — fried, roasted, baked, poached, sautéed, grilled, steamed, simmered or smoked. The options are virtually endless.

BUYING TIPS

- Chicken meat should be firm and plump with no noticeable odor, and there should be no liquid accumulated on the tray.
- Press on the breastbone — it should give easily if chicken is young and tender.
- Cold raw chicken should be used within a few days of purchase. The "sell-by" date is 7 days after the bird was processed and is the final day for store sale.

- Chicken breasts are available with skin and bone, skinless with bone, and skinless and boneless.
- 1½ lb. = approximately 4 chicken breast halves

FREEZING AND THAWING TIPS

- To freeze, either seal in freezer bags or carefully wrap in foil or freezer paper.
- For best results, storage time in the freezer for raw chicken should not exceed 3 to 6 months.
- Thaw chicken before cooking.
- Thaw frozen chicken, covered, in the refrigerator.
- Cook all chicken immediately after thawing.
- Cooked chicken should not be frozen more than 1 month.

BONING A CHICKEN BREAST (using a whole breast)

1. Remove skin and place the breast meat side down.

2. With the tip of a knife, cut through the membrane covering the breastbone. Pick up the breast with both hands and press back on the ribs to break them away from the breastbone. Pull out the breastbone, including cartilage.

3. Cut away ribs: slip your fingers between ribs and meat and work the meat free from the bone, or use a knife and make shallow cuts to separate the meat from the bone.

4. Split the breast in half, removing tough membranes lying along the breastbone.

5. As an extra refinement, remove tendon from breast meat: hold one end of the tendon on the work surface and, with a knife, scrape from the end of the tendon inward to remove.

POACHING CHICKEN BREASTS

1. Trim off any excess fat and place chicken in large saucepan.

2. For every pound of meat, add 1 chopped carrot, 1 chopped celery stalk and ½ chopped onion. Add enough cold water to cover.

3. Add a "bouquet garni": 3 sprigs fresh parsley, 2 sprigs fresh thyme and 1 bay leaf placed in a square of cheesecloth and tied with a string for easy removal.

4. Bring slowly to a boil, skim, reduce heat to medium low and simmer gently, covered, for approximately 6 to 7 minutes.

5. Remove chicken breasts from the saucepan and set aside to cool. When cool, remove meat from bones.

BEST METHOD FOR FRYING CHICKEN

1. Soak chicken pieces in liquid such as buttermilk, milk or water.

2. Roll in seasoned flour (seasoning usually consists of salt, pepper and/or seasonings of choice).

3. In a skillet, heat about 1½ inches of oil to 350°F. and add chicken.

4. Cook until golden brown on both sides and almost done, about 15 minutes.

5. Raise heat to medium-high, 375°, and finish browning, about 5 minutes longer.

6. Drain and serve immediately.

SIX STEPS TO A SUCCESSFUL SAUTÉ

1. Choose a pan of the right size so that the meat just fills the pan.

2. Cook in very hot fat so the surface of the meat is "seized" and forms a crust that retains the juices inside the meat.

3.   Use just enough fat so that it circulates freely under the food (too much fat will give the effect of deep frying).

4.   Discard excess fat before adding liquid to the pan.

5.   Traditionally, cooking is finished on top of the stove, but less attention is needed if a sauté is put in a 350° oven. (Be sure handle of sauté pan can withstand the heat).

6.   If a sauté starts to dry out before the meat is cooked, add a little more liquid and cover the pan. If, on the other hand, the meat is cooked before the sauce is properly reduced, transfer the meat to a dish to keep warm and boil the sauce down to the proper consistency.

INDIAN CHICKEN TRIANGLES

*This spicy appetizer can be made ahead of time
and frozen. To clarify butter, melt and skim off milky layers.*

1 lb. chicken breast, poached
2 tbs. butter
1 small onion, diced
1 cup diced mushrooms
1 tsp. ground cumin

2 tbs. minced parsley
salt and pepper to taste
1 pkg. (1 lb.) phyllo dough
1 lb. butter, melted and clarified

Finely dice poached chicken and set aside. Melt butter in a skillet and sauté onion and mushrooms until limp. Add chicken, cumin, parsley, salt and pepper and stir. Taste and adjust seasonings. Lightly brush a phyllo sheet all over with butter. Cut phyllo into 4 strips and fold each strip in half. Brush folded strip with butter and place 1 tsp. chicken mixture in one corner. Fold into a triangle and continue folding in this fashion (flag fold) until strip is used. Brush resulting triangle packet with butter and place on a cookie sheet with sides. Repeat with remaining phyllo and filling. Bake at 350° for 20 minutes or until golden brown.

Makes 36

CHICKEN SATEH

This extremely popular appetizer originated in Thailand. Check Oriental grocery sources; if lemon grass or lime leaves are unavailable use lemon or lime juices instead.

2 lb. chicken breast meat, skinned
6 tbs. vegetable oil
2 tbs. lemon juice
4-5 cloves garlic, minced

¾ tsp. red pepper flakes
2 tbs. curry powder
2 tsp. sugar
2 tsp. fish sauce

SATEH SAUCE

¼ cup vegetable oil
2 cloves garlic, minced
1 onion, chopped
½ tsp. chili powder
3 lime leaves, or 1 tbs. lime juice
½ tsp. curry powder
1 tbs. chopped lemon grass, or
  1-2 tbs. lemon juice
1 cup coconut milk

½ cup milk
¼ tsp. cinnamon
3 bay leaves
2 tsp. tamarind paste, or 2 tbs.
  lemon juice
2 tbs. fish sauce
3 tbs. dark brown sugar
3 tbs. lemon juice
1 cup chunky peanut butter

Cut chicken into thin strips and thread onto bamboo skewers*. In a food processor or blender, combine oil, lemon juice, garlic, red pepper flakes, curry powder, sugar and fish sauce and blend until well mixed. Pour mixture over chicken and marinate for at least 2 hours.

Make sauce. In a saucepan, heat oil and add garlic, onion, chili powder, lime leaves, curry powder and lemon grass and cook for 2 minutes. Stir in coconut milk and remaining ingredients. Reduce heat and simmer for 30 minutes.

Just before serving, broil or grill chicken until cooked through, about 4 to 5 minutes on each side. Serve with hot *Sateh Sauce*.

Makes 10-12 servings

*Soak bamboo skewers in water for about 20 minutes so they won't burn.

CHICKEN APPETIZER SWIRLS

*Here's another great appetizer that can be made
ahead of time. Garnish with a sprig of cilantro.*

8 oz. cooked chicken breast
4 tsp. mango chutney
2 tbs. mayonnaise
¼ cup chopped green bell pepper
4 green onions, chopped
4 gherkin pickles, chopped

½ tsp. curry powder
salt and pepper to taste
6 slices bread, crust removed
⅓ cup butter, softened
24 pimiento-stuffed green olives
cilantro sprigs for garnish

Chop chicken into a very fine mince. In a bowl, combine chicken, chutney, mayonnaise, green pepper, green onions, gherkins, curry, salt and pepper, mixing well. Taste and adjust seasonings. With a rolling pin, flatten bread slices. Butter bread and spread with chicken mixture. Arrange a row of whole stuffed green olives along the short edge of each slice. Roll up jelly roll style. Wrap in plastic wrap and chill for 2 hours. Cut each roll into 4 slices at a slight angle. Garnish with a sprig of cilantro.

Makes 24

BAKED CHICKEN WON TONS

*A vegetable and chicken filling is wrapped in won
ton wrappers and baked instead of deep fried.*

8 oz. chicken breast meat, skinned
1/4 cup chopped celery
1/2 cup shredded carrot
1 tbs. soy sauce
1 tbs. dry sherry
2 tsp. grated ginger root

2 tsp. cornstarch
1/3 cup bottled plum sauce or
  sweet and sour sauce
24 square won ton wrappers
3-4 tbs. melted butter

In a food processor or meat grinder, chop chicken breast into a fine grind. Place chicken in a bowl and add remaining ingredients, except wrappers and butter. Stir to combine. Fill each won ton with about 1 rounded tsp. filling. Moisten edges with water and pinch opposite ends closed. Seal. Brush bottom and sides generously with butter. Place on a baking sheet and bake at 375° for 10 minutes or until brown and crisp.

Makes 24

11

WALNUT SESAME CHICKEN

*This delicious, crispy appetizer is coated with a
walnut sesame batter, fried, sprinkled with a fragrant salt and
pepper mixture and served with a tangy sweet and sour sauce.*

1 lb. chicken breast meat, skinned
1 tsp. salt
1 egg white
1 tbs. cornstarch
1 cup very finely chopped walnuts

5-6 tbs. sesame seeds
oil for deep frying
3 tbs. salt
2 tsp. Szechwan peppercorns

Freeze chicken partially and slice across the grain at an angle into thin, long pieces. Combine 1 tsp. salt, egg white and cornstarch together and mix until smooth. Add chicken, stir and set aside. Mix walnuts and sesame seeds together. Coat chicken with walnut mixture, lay out on waxed paper and refrigerate for 1 hour before frying. In a small skillet over medium heat, add 3 tbs. salt and peppercorns. Stir until pepper begins to smoke slightly and salt turns slightly brown. Remove from heat and crush with a mortar and pestle.

Heat oil to 350°. Add chicken pieces in batches, without crowding. Fry until golden brown and drain on paper towels. Sprinkle with salt-pepper mixture. Cut chicken into bite-sized pieces. Serve with *Sweet and Sour Sauce*.

SWEET AND SOUR SAUCE

1½ tbs. white vinegar
1 tbs. honey
1 tsp. soy sauce
1 tbs. tomato paste
¼ cup hot water

1 tbs. vegetable oil
1 clove garlic, minced
¼ tsp. grated ginger root
1 tsp. cornstarch
1 tbs. water

In a bowl, combine vinegar, honey, soy sauce, tomato paste and hot water. In a saucepan, heat oil and cook garlic and ginger for 1 minute over medium heat, but do not let garlic turn brown. Add vinegar mixture and bring to a boil. Mix cornstarch with 1 tbs. water, add to saucepan and stir until mixture thickens.

Makes 8-12 servings

ORIENTAL CHICKEN ROLLS

These appetizers can be make ahead of time and
frozen. Then just before serving, deep fry and serve immediately.

2 whole cooked chicken breasts, boned and skinned
1 can (8 oz.) water chestnuts, drained and minced
$\frac{1}{2}$ cup minced mushrooms
4 green onions, minced
2 tbs. cornstarch
2 tsp. soy sauce
2 tsp. sesame oil
1 tsp. white vinegar
1 tsp. sugar
1 tsp. salt
1 tsp. dry sherry
20 phyllo sheets
melted butter for brushing
1 egg, beaten
oil for deep frying

Place cooked chicken in a food processor or meat grinder and grind coarsely. In a bowl, combine ground chicken, water chestnuts, mushrooms, onions, cornstarch, soy sauce, sesame oil, vinegar, sugar, salt and sherry, mixing well. Cut phyllo sheets into 2 equal strips lengthwise. Brush with melted butter and fold in half lengthwise. Brush again with melted butter and place about 1 tbs. filling near the end. Roll into a cylinder shape, folding sides in, and seal with a little beaten egg. Heat oil to 350° and fry until browned; drain on paper towels. Serve immediately.

Makes 40

CHICKEN EMPANADAS

*Puff pastry sheets are now available in the frozen
food section of the grocery store. Easy pastry shells ideal for
appetizers can be made by cutting the pastry into squares and lining
miniature muffin tins.*

2 pkg. (17¼ oz. each) frozen
 puff pastry sheets
⅓ cup raisins
1 cup hot water
3 tbs. vegetable oil
⅔ cup minced onion
1 lb. chicken breast meat, skinned
3 tbs. chopped green olives

¾ tsp. red pepper flakes
1-1½ tsp. salt
1 tsp. ground cumin
¼ tsp. cinnamon
2 tbs. butter
2 tbs. flour
1 cup chicken broth
½ cup chopped slivered almonds

Lay out puff pastry sheets to defrost while preparing filling. Soak raisins in hot water for 10 minutes; drain. Heat oil in a skillet and sauté onion until soft. Finely dice chicken meat and add to onion mixture with olives, red pepper flakes, salt, cumin and cinnamon. Cook over medium heat until chicken is no longer pink, about 5 minutes.

Heat butter in a saucepan, add flour and stir for 1 minute. Add chicken broth and stir until thickened. Add to chicken mixture and set aside until mixture is cool. Cut the 10-inch square of puff pastry into 16 pieces and line miniature muffin cups. Place about 1 tbs. filling in each cup and sprinkle with chopped almonds. Bake in a 375° oven for about 15 to 20 minutes or until pastry is golden brown and puffed.

Makes about 60

CHICKEN SPREAD

A very simple chicken spread, this goes well with crackers, served on bread rounds or used as a sandwich filling. If you spread it on bread rounds, it's nice to garnish with chopped olives or chopped red bell pepper.

1½ cups minced cooked chicken breast meat
½ cup almonds, toasted
2 tbs. cream
2 tbs. softened butter
2 tbs. white wine or sherry
salt and white pepper to taste

Place all ingredients in a food processor or blender and process until smooth. Chill mixture thoroughly before serving.

Makes 2 cups

18

CURRIED CHICKEN FILLING OR SPREAD

*This filling can be used in baked puff pastry shells
or as a spread for crackers or bread. If you don't like curry,
substitute Dijon mustard for the curry powder.*

2½ cups diced cooked chicken breast meat
1 tbs. minced green onion tops
8 oz. cream cheese or butter
½ tsp. curry powder, or to taste
1 tsp. lemon juice
salt and white pepper to taste

Place all ingredients in a food processor or blender and blend with a pulsing action until either slightly chunky or smooth, as you prefer. Chill until ready to serve.

Makes 3 cups

WALNUT CHICKEN SPREAD

*Consider serving this piped onto vegetables like
split snow peas or endive leaves. Or serve it as a cracker
spread or vegetable dip.*

2 whole chicken breasts, cooked,
  boned and skinned
2/3 cup mayonnaise
2/3 cup sour cream (can use
  nonfat)
1/4 cup lemon juice
1/2 cup minced onion, or to taste

3 cloves garlic, minced
1 tsp. salt
1/4 tsp. Tabasco Sauce, or more
  to taste
1 cup walnuts, toasted
1/4 cup chopped parsley

Cut cooked chicken into cubes and place in a food processor or
blender. Add remaining ingredients and blend until well mixed. Taste
and adjust seasonings. Chill for several hours before using.

Makes 2 cups

CREAMY TROPICAL CHICKEN SALAD

*Chill for 2 or 3 hours to blend the flavors. Serve on a
bed of shredded lettuce and garnish with orange slices and a few
maraschino cherries.*

1 can (14 oz.) sweetened
  condensed milk
1 cup plain yogurt
1 cup fresh or frozen lemon juice
½ tsp. salt
½ tsp. curry powder

3 cups diced poached chicken
  breast meat
2 cups finely chopped celery
1 can (11 oz.) mandarin oranges,
  drained
1 cup slivered almonds, toasted

In a bowl, combine condensed milk, yogurt, lemon juice, salt and
curry together and mix well. Add chicken, celery and oranges and gently
fold to mix. Taste and adjust seasonings. Chill for 2 or 3 hours. Just
before serving, add toasted almonds.

Makes 8 servings

CHUTNEY CHICKEN SALAD

This version of chicken salad is easy to fix. Serve
with crusty bread and a vegetable accompaniment.

3 lb. chicken breasts, poached
3 cups diced celery
1 bunch green onions, sliced
1 cup drained pineapple tidbits
6 cups mayonnaise
1/2 jar (12 oz.) mango chutney

1/2 cup fresh or frozen lemon
 juice
1 tbs. curry powder
1 1/2 tsp. salt
1 cup slivered almonds, toasted

Skin poached chicken, dice into 1/2-inch chunks and place in a large bowl. Add celery, green onions and pineapple tidbits; set aside. In a separate bowl, combine mayonnaise, chutney, lemon juice, curry powder and salt. Add enough mayonnaise dressing to moisten chicken mixture and stir gently. Taste and adjust seasonings. Refrigerate until ready to serve. Just before serving, add slivered almonds.

Makes 9 servings

CHICKEN PASTA SALAD

You can create endless variety by using different vegetables.

2 whole boned chicken breasts
1 cup chicken broth
1/4 cup white wine
salt and pepper to taste
2 cups mayonnaise, or as needed
2 cloves garlic, minced
juice of 1 lemon
1 tsp. Dijon mustard
salt and pepper to taste

1 lb. pasta (fusilli, bows or shells), cooked
1 cup provolone cheese chunks
1 cup cooked green beans
1 cup chopped seeded tomatoes
1 cup chopped celery
4 green onions, sliced
1/2 cup black olives, sliced in half
1/4 cup pine nuts, toasted

Poach chicken in chicken broth, wine, salt and pepper for 6 to 7 minutes, remove from liquid and cool. Cut into 1-inch chunks. In a food processor or blender, blend mayonnaise, garlic, lemon juice, mustard, salt and pepper until smooth. Mix chicken chunks, dressing, pasta and remaining ingredients, except pine nuts, together. Taste and adjust seasonings. Add pine nuts just before serving.

Makes 10 servings

CHICKEN, AVOCADO AND PAPAYA SALAD

Vary this easy-to-make, refreshing salad by using mangos instead of papayas. Chive blossoms or fresh flowers along the edge of the plate make a beautiful and elegant presentation.

3 whole chicken breasts,
   poached and skinned
3 avocados, sliced (prefer Haas
   variety)
3 ripe papayas, peeled and sliced
1 lb. mixed salad greens
½ cup orange juice

1 tbs. grated orange peel (zest)
2 tbs. minced fresh tarragon
1 egg, or ¼ cup cream
3 tbs. vinegar (prefer balsamic)
1 clove garlic, minced
salt and pepper to taste
1 cup vegetable oil

Cut cooked chicken into slivers and chill. On individual plates, arrange chicken, avocado slices and papaya slices on a bed of mixed salad greens. Chill until ready to serve. In a food processor or blender, combine orange juice, orange zest, tarragon, egg, vinegar, garlic, salt and pepper and blend until well mixed. Slowly add oil in a thin stream while machine is running. Spoon over salad just before serving.

Makes 6-8 servings

HOT CHICKEN NIÇOISE SALAD

This is a hot chicken salad that should be served over rice. Serve it with a good wholesome bread.

1 tbs. olive oil
2 cloves garlic, minced
1 can (8½ oz.) artichokes,
  drained and halved
1 can (6 oz.) pitted black olives
1 can (1 lb.) whole tomatoes,
  with juice

1 tsp. dried tarragon
½ cup chicken broth
½ cup dry white wine
3 whole chicken breasts,
  poached and skinned

Heat oil in a skillet and sauté garlic until soft but not brown. Add artichokes and olives and sauté briefly. Cut tomatoes into quarters and add to pan with tarragon, chicken broth and wine. Simmer for 5 minutes. Cut chicken breast meat into thin slivers, add to pan and heat just until hot. Serve over rice.

Makes 6 servings

CHINESE CHICKEN SALAD

The unusual ingredient in this salad is the noodles.
Rice noodles (mai fun) are quickly deep fried
and turned to crispy white strands.

1/4 cup soy sauce
2 tbs. mirin (sweet rice cooking wine)
1/2 tsp. ground ginger
2 tbs. sugar
2 cloves garlic, minced
3 whole chicken breasts, boned and skinned

oil for deep frying
1 pkg. (8 oz.) thin rice noodles
2 heads iceberg lettuce
3 green onions, chopped
Dressing, follows
3 tbs. sesame seeds, toasted
1 cup slivered almonds, toasted

In a bowl, mix soy sauce, mirin, ginger, sugar and garlic together. Cut chicken into large slivers, add to bowl, stir to coat and marinate in the refrigerator for at least 1 hour. Once chicken has marinated, quickly sauté until cooked and cut into small pieces. Chill until ready to use.

Heat oil to 375°, break up noodles and drop small amounts in oil. The noodles will cook and expand almost immediately. As soon as noodles stop expanding, remove from oil and drain on paper towels. Continue until all noodles have been fried.

To assemble salad, shred lettuce and place in a large bowl. Add chicken pieces and green onions. Toss with dressing. Gently stir in sesame seeds, almonds and noodles and serve immediately.

DRESSING

6 tbs. sugar
2 tsp. salt
1/4 tsp. pepper

1/4 cup vegetable oil
1/4 cup rice vinegar
2 tbs. lemon juice

Blend ingredients.

Makes 6-8 servings

SESAME CHICKEN SALAD

Sesame-coated chicken and colorful vegetables make a unique salad.

2½ lb. chicken breasts, boned and skinned
flour seasoned with salt and pepper
1 egg, beaten
½ cup sesame seeds
oil for deep frying
salt to taste
1 lb. mixed salad greens

2 carrots, peeled and cut into matchstick strips
½ red bell pepper, cut into fine strips
½ small red onion, cut into fine shreds
3 tbs. chopped cilantro
Soy Dressing, follows

Cut whole chicken breasts in half and cut each half into 4 strips. Dredge strips in seasoned flour, coat with beaten egg and roll in sesame seeds. Heat oil to 375° and quickly fry to golden brown. Remove chicken from oil with a slotted spoon and drain on paper towels. Lightly sprinkle with a little salt and allow to cool.

Place salad greens on individual plates. Sprinkle with carrots, red pepper strips, red onion and cilantro. Drizzle *Soy Dressing* over vegetables and arrange chicken strips in a star pattern on top of vegetables.

Makes 6 servings

SOY DRESSING

1/2 cup soy sauce
1/4 cup toasted sesame oil
3-4 cloves garlic, minced
2 tbs. minced ginger root
1 tsp. sugar

In a food processor or blender, blend soy sauce, sesame oil, garlic, ginger root and sugar. Taste and adjust seasonings.

PASTA SALAD WITH CHICKEN AND VEGETABLES

Seafood such as crabmeat and/or shrimp can be substituted for the chicken in this recipe. Refrigerate for at least an hour before serving to allow the pasta to absorb the flavors.

1 lb. spiral pasta
12 oz. cooked chicken breast
  meat, skinned
½ lb. snow peas, blanched
1 head broccoli florets, blanched

1 pt. cherry tomatoes, halved
1 can (6 oz.) sliced water
  chestnuts, drained
Dressing, follows

Cook pasta according to package directions and drain. Cut chicken into small cubes and place in a large bowl with cooked pasta. Add snow peas, broccoli, tomatoes and water chestnuts; mix. Add as much dressing to salad as you desire and refrigerate for several hours before serving.

Makes 8 servings

DRESSING

1 egg, or ¼ cup cream
¼ cup red wine vinegar
½ tsp. salt
¼ tsp. pepper
½ tsp. sugar

2 tbs. chopped fresh parsley
2 tsp. dill
1 tsp. basil
1-2 cloves garlic, minced
1 cup vegetable oil

In a food processor or blender, place remaining ingredients, except oil. Blend to mix. With machine running, slowly pour in oil in a thin stream until all oil is incorporated and dressing thickens. Taste and adjust seasonings.

SPANISH CHICKEN SALAD

This salad is made with a salsa vinaigrette. The
oranges and red onions create a beautiful color combination.

⅓ cup vegetable oil
¼ cup red wine vinegar (prefer balsamic)
1½ tsp. sugar
½ tsp. garlic salt
¼ tsp. pepper
¼ tsp. ground cumin
⅔ cup bottled chunky taco salsa

2 large oranges, peeled and cut into rings
1 small jicama, peeled
½ red onion, peeled and thinly sliced
1½ lb. poached chicken breasts
1 head butterleaf lettuce

In a food processor or blender, process oil, vinegar, sugar, garlic salt, pepper and cumin until well mixed. Stir in salsa. Cut orange rings into quarters and cut jicama into thin matchstick strips. Separate onion slices into rings. Shred or dice poached chicken. Tear lettuce into bite-sized pieces and place on plates. Toss remaining ingredients with dressing and arrange on top of lettuce. Serve immediately.

Makes 6 servings

GRAPE AND CHICKEN SALAD

*You can vary the flavor and appearance of this
salad by using different varieties of grapes. The flavor can change
greatly by using alternative vinegars such as raspberry or tarragon.
It's pretty garnished with fresh flowers.*

4-5 cups diced cooked, skinned
  chicken breast meat
4 stalks celery, chopped
1 cup red or black seedless grapes
1 cup green seedless grapes
⅓ cup nonfat sour cream

1½ tbs. red wine vinegar (prefer
  balsamic)
1½ tbs. brown sugar
salt and pepper to taste
2-3 tbs. milk
1 head lettuce, finely shredded

Place chicken in a bowl with celery. Cut grapes in half and add to chicken. Mix sour cream, vinegar, brown sugar, salt, pepper and enough milk to thin to desired consistency. Pour dressing over salad and refrigerate until ready to serve. To serve, place shredded lettuce on individual plates and spoon chicken salad on top.

Makes 6 servings

SIX QUICK WAYS TO COOK
A CHICKEN BREAST

Use one of these special treatments for grilled, broiled or baked chicken breasts. (Bake in a 350° oven for 30 minutes or less.)

LEMON BASIL BUTTER

Makes ½ cup

6 tbs. butter, softened
2-3 tbs. chopped fresh basil
salt to taste

½ tsp. pepper
1 tbs. chopped lemon peel (zest)
few drops lemon juice to taste

Cream butter with remaining ingredients. Melt and brush on chicken before baking or broiling. Or, chill butter in a cylinder shape, slice into rounds and serve on top of cooked chicken breasts.

JAZZED-UP TERIYAKI

Makes 2½ cups

1 cup bottled teriyaki sauce
1½ cups honey
1 tsp. ground ginger

½ tsp. chopped garlic
toasted sesame seeds for garnish

Combine ingredients and brush over chicken breasts before cooking. Sprinkle cooked chicken with sesame seeds.

PEANUT BUTTER MARINADE

Makes 2¼ cups

2 tbs. vegetable oil
½ cup finely chopped onion
1 clove garlic, minced
½ tsp. cayenne pepper
1 tsp. salt

½ cup creamy peanut butter
2 tbs. soy sauce
2 tbs. lemon juice
1 cup water

Heat oil in a saucepan and sauté onion, garlic and cayenne for several minutes. Stir in remaining ingredients and cook over low heat for 5 minutes. Cool. Marinate chicken in sauce for 1 hour. Baste while cooking.

SPICY BARBECUE GLAZE

Makes 2 cups

1¼ cups ketchup
6 tbs. honey
¼ cup Worcestershire sauce

2 tbs. vinegar
2 tsp. mustard
dash Tabasco Sauce, optional

Whisk ingredients together and brush over chicken breasts before cooking. Baste frequently with glaze.

ORIENTAL SAUCE

Makes 1¼ cups

2 tbs. cornstarch mixed with ¼
  cup cold water
1 cup chicken stock
1 tbs. vegetable oil
1 tbs. dry sherry

1 tsp. sugar
1 tbs. soy sauce
1 tbs. oyster sauce
½ tsp. sesame oil
salt to taste

Cook ingredients over medium heat for several minutes, stirring constantly, until mixture thickens. Pour over cooked chicken breasts.

CITRUS MARINADE

Makes 1½ cups

¼ cup orange juice
¼ cup lime juice
¼ cup lemon juice
¼ cup olive oil
2-3 tsp. red pepper flakes

1 tsp. chili powder
1 tsp. ground cumin
1 tbs. salt
dash pepper
2 onions, finely chopped

Whisk ingredients together. Marinate chicken breasts in mixture for at least 12 hours. Cook as desired, basting frequently with marinade.

GRILLED BASIL CHICKEN

*Basil is used to baste the chicken as well as to
make a basil butter sauce to serve as an accompaniment.*

¾ tsp. freshly ground pepper
2 whole chicken breasts, skinned
  and halved
⅓ cup melted butter
½ cup chopped fresh basil

½ cup softened butter
2 tbs. grated Parmesan cheese
2 cloves garlic, minced
¼ tsp. salt
⅛ tsp. pepper

Press pepper into chicken breasts. Mix melted butter with ¼ cup of the chopped basil. Brush chicken breast with butter mixture. In a mixing bowl, combine softened butter, remaining ¼ cup chopped basil, Parmesan, garlic, salt and pepper; beat until well blended. Grill chicken for about 8 minutes per side, basting well with melted butter mixture. Place chicken on a platter and serve with basil butter.

Makes 4 servings

CASHEW CHICKEN WITH BROCCOLI

*This healthy stir-fry takes just minutes to cook once
the vegetables are prepared. Serve with steaming hot rice.*

½ cup chicken broth
1 tbs. cornstarch
3 tbs. dry sherry
2 tbs. soy sauce
¼ tsp. Tabasco Sauce
3 whole chicken breasts
¼ cup vegetable oil
2-3 slices ginger root
3 cups broccoli florets
1 red bell pepper, cut into 1-inch squares
½ lb. mushrooms, sliced
1 bunch green onions, minced
1-2 cloves garlic, minced
⅓ cup dry roasted cashews

In a bowl, combine chicken broth, cornstarch, sherry, soy sauce and Tabasco. Skin, bone and cut chicken breasts into 1-inch chunks. Heat about 3 tbs. of the oil in a wok or skillet and add sliced ginger root and chicken. Cook, stirring constantly, until chicken just turns white. Remove chicken from wok and discard ginger root. Add remaining oil and place broccoli, red pepper, mushrooms, green onions and garlic in wok or skillet. Cook for 3 minutes, stirring constantly. Return chicken to wok and add cornstarch mixture, stirring until sauce thickens slightly. Sprinkle with cashews and serve immediately.

Makes 6-8 servings

CHICKEN A LA CHEVRE

This chicken breast stuffed with a creamy goat cheese mixture is very elegant and easy to fix. Green peppercorns are an acquired taste, so they are an optional ingredient. Top with Mushroom Sauce and serve with rice.

⅔ cup red currant jelly
⅓ cup port wine
2 pkg. (⅞ oz. each) Knorr Swiss Hunter Sauce mix
1½ cups water
3 tbs. green peppercorns, optional
4 oz. chevre cheese (goat cheese)
4 whole chicken breasts, skinned, boned and halved
Mushroom Sauce, follows

Combine red currant jelly, wine, Hunter Sauce mix, water and peppercorns in a saucepan and bring to a boil. Reduce heat and simmer for 2 minutes. Remove from heat and combine cheese with ¼ cup of sauce (remaining sauce will be used for basting). With a sharp knife, cut a pocket in the side of each breast half. Divide cheese mixture equally to fill pockets. Place on a rack in a shallow roasting pan. Bake at 375° for 20 minutes, basting with sauce as chicken cooks. Serve topped with *Mushroom Sauce.*

MUSHROOM SAUCE

½ cup butter
¼ cup sliced mushrooms
¼ cup flour
¼ cup white wine

1 cup cream
2 tsp. tarragon
salt and pepper to taste

Melt butter in a heavy saucepan and sauté mushrooms until tender. Stir in flour and cook for 1 minute. Add wine, cream and tarragon and stir until thickened. Add salt and pepper to taste.

Makes 8 servings

CRAB-STUFFED CHICKEN BREASTS

*These chicken breasts are stuffed with a creamy
mushroom and crab mixture that is topped with Swiss cheese.*

4 whole chicken breasts
⅓ cup sliced green onions
⅓ cup sliced mushrooms
¼ cup butter
3 tbs. flour
½ tsp. dried thyme
¾ cup chicken stock
½ cup milk
⅓ cup dry white wine
1 cup grated Swiss cheese
salt and pepper to taste
1 cup crabmeat
2 tbs. chopped fresh parsley
⅓ cup fine dry breadcrumbs
½ cup sliced almonds

Skin, bone and halve chicken breasts; pound to ¼-inch thick. In a skillet, sauté green onions and mushrooms in butter until soft. Stir in flour and thyme. Add chicken stock, milk, wine, ½ of the cheese, salt and pepper. Cook over medium heat until thickened. Remove sauce from heat.

Combine ¼ cup sauce with crab, parsley and breadcrumbs. Divide mixture evenly on chicken breasts. Roll breasts, secure with toothpicks if desired and place in a buttered baking dish. Pour remaining sauce over rolled breasts. Bake in a 350° oven for 30 minutes. Sprinkle with remaining cheese and sliced almonds. Bake 10 minutes longer and serve immediately.

Makes 8 servings

BROCCOLI AND CHICKEN QUICHE

It's perfect for breakfast, brunch or lunch with a fruit salad.

CRUST

1⅓ cups flour
½ cup cold butter
1 tsp. salt
¼ cup ice water

Using a food processor or pastry blender, quickly mix together flour, ½ cup butter and salt until mixture resembles coarse crumbs. Add water and process (or stir) mixture together and form into a ball. Cover with plastic wrap and refrigerate while preparing filling.

FILLING

2 tbs. butter
10 medium mushrooms, sliced
1 small onion, diced
8 oz. cooked chicken breast meat
1 pkg. (10 oz.) frozen chopped broccoli
4 large eggs
1½ cups cream
1 tsp. salt
¼ tsp. nutmeg
¼ tsp. crumbled dried tarragon
4 oz. Gruyère or Swiss cheese, grated

Melt 2 tbs. butter in a skillet and sauté mushrooms and onion until soft; set aside. Finely dice cooked chicken. Defrost and squeeze broccoli dry. Using a mixer or food processor, blend together eggs, cream, salt, nutmeg and tarragon.

Roll chilled pastry dough into a circle and line a 10-inch pie pan or quiche pan. Place a piece of parchment paper over pastry dough and fill cavity with dry beans. Bake at 450° for 10 minutes. Remove pastry from oven and remove paper and beans.

Sprinkle 1/2 of the cheese in bottom of partially baked crust. Cover with broccoli and sprinkle with diced chicken. Evenly distribute mushroom-onion mixture over chicken. Pour egg mixture on top and sprinkle with remaining grated cheese. Bake at 450° for 10 minutes. Reduce temperature to 325° and bake for 20 to 25 minutes more or until filling is browned and firm. Let stand at least 10 minutes before serving.

Makes 6-8 servings

POLYNESIAN MANGO CHICKEN

A delicious, fresh sauce made from mangos and papaya is poured over baked chicken breasts. Serve with a vegetable salad and rice pilaf.

8 chicken breast halves, with skin
8 lemon slices
½ cup diced onion
salt and pepper to taste
2 ripe mangos, diced

1 ripe papaya, diced
1 jalapeño chile, diced, or to taste
2 tsp. soy sauce
3 tbs. lemon juice
2 tbs. chopped chives

Lay chicken breasts out on a baking sheet. Loosen skin and place 1 lemon slice and some diced onion under each skin. Season outside with salt and pepper. Place in a 375° oven and bake for 20 minutes. Using a food processor or blender, process mangos, papaya, jalapeno, soy sauce, lemon juice and chives until a coarse mix is formed. Pour sauce over chicken and serve.

Makes 8 servings

CHICKEN WITH RED PEPPER SAUCE

This sauce recipe can be made ahead of time. Just before serving, quickly sauté the chicken and reheat the sauce.

6 chicken breast halves, boned
  and skinned
salt and pepper to taste
1/4 cup olive oil
2 cloves garlic, minced
1/2 small onion, chopped

2 red bell peppers, chopped
1 tbs. vermouth
1/4 tsp. Tabasco Sauce
2-3 tbs. cream
1/4 cup chopped cilantro

Pound breasts to flatten. Season with salt and pepper and set aside. In a saucepan, heat 2 tbs. of the oil. Add garlic, onion, peppers, vermouth and Tabasco and simmer. Cover and cook for about 25 minutes, until vegetables are soft. Put mixture into a food processor or blender and puree. Add cream and blend to mix. Heat remaining oil in a skillet, sear chicken over medium-high heat, reduce heat and cook until just done, about 5 to 6 minutes. To serve, coat plate with red pepper sauce, cut chicken into strips, place over sauce and sprinkle with cilantro.

Makes 6 servings

SPINACH-STUFFED CHICKEN

*Onion and bacon make a great accompaniment to
spinach for this delicious stuffing. Serve with scalloped potatoes.*

½ lb. bacon, diced
1 large onion, chopped
1 pkg. (10 oz.) frozen chopped
spinach, thawed
1 egg
½ cup breadcrumbs

¼ cup grated Parmesan cheese
1 tbs. chopped pimiento
salt and pepper to taste
6 chicken breast halves, boned,
with skin
2 tbs. butter, melted

Fry bacon in a skillet and drain on paper towels. Remove all but 2 tbs. bacon drippings from pan and sauté onion until tender. Squeeze defrosted spinach dry. Add spinach to onion mixture with egg, breadcrumbs, Parmesan, pimiento, salt and pepper. Stir to mix. Lift skin from each breast half and fill with stuffing. Fold edges under to make a compact bundle. Brush with melted butter and place in a baking pan. Bake at 350° for 20 to 30 minutes, or until done. Serve whole or cut into attractive slices.

Makes 6 servings

DIJON CHICKEN

Great for picnics! Serve it hot or cold.

8 chicken breast halves, skinned
1/4-1/2 cup Dijon mustard
salt and pepper to taste
1 cup sour cream
1 cup seasoned breadcrumbs
2-3 tbs. melted butter

Cover a baking sheet with foil and grease lightly. Thinly coat each chicken piece with mustard and sprinkle with salt and pepper. Allow to sit for 30 minutes to marinate. Gently spread sour cream over chicken pieces and roll in breadcrumbs. Place pieces a few inches apart on baking sheet. Bake at 375° for 20 minutes. Drip melted butter over each piece. Return to oven for an additional 25 minutes or until golden brown and tender. Drain on paper towels.

Makes 8 servings

HAWAIIAN CHICKEN

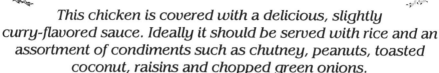

This chicken is covered with a delicious, slightly curry-flavored sauce. Ideally it should be served with rice and an assortment of condiments such as chutney, peanuts, toasted coconut, raisins and chopped green onions.

3 lb. chicken breasts, skinned and boned
1 cup water
2 celery tops, chopped
2 onions, thinly sliced
1½ tsp. salt
2 cucumbers, peeled and seeded
1 green bell pepper
¼ cup butter
2 cloves garlic, minced
2 medium apples, peeled, cored and diced
2 tomatoes, peeled and chopped
2 tbs. flour
½ tsp. thyme
⅓ tsp. cinnamon
1 tbs. curry powder
1 tbs. sugar
2 tsp. salt
1 cup chicken broth
½ cup cream
⅓ cup white wine

Place chicken breasts in a baking dish. Add water, celery tops, ½ of the onions and 1½ tsp. salt. Butter waxed paper and place over chicken, buttered side down. Bake at 350° for 25 minutes or until chicken is tender. Remove from oven, remove chicken from liquid and cool. Cut meat into bite-sized pieces; set aside.

Cut cucumbers into thin matchstick strips. Cut pepper into 2-inch-long slivers. Melt ½ of the butter in a skillet and sauté cucumbers and green peppers until slightly wilted but still crisp.

In a saucepan, melt remaining butter and sauté remaining onions with garlic, apples and tomatoes until soft. Add flour and stir for 2 minutes. Add thyme, cinnamon, curry, sugar, 2 tsp. salt, chicken broth, cream and wine. Simmer for 5 minutes.

Before serving, place chicken, cucumbers and green peppers together in a large saucepan. Gently stir in sauce and heat. Serve with rice and condiments.

Makes 6 servings

BAKED CHICKEN WITH MUSHROOMS

You can't go wrong with bacon and mushrooms.

8 chicken breast halves, skinned
8 slices bacon
½ lb. mushrooms, sliced
½ tsp. salt
pepper to taste

½ cup butter, melted
¼ cup flour
¾ cup chicken broth
¼ cup dry white wine
½ cup cream

Use bacon to wrap mushrooms around chicken breasts and secure with toothpicks. Sprinkle with salt and pepper. Pour ½ of the butter in a baking dish, place chicken in dish and drizzle with remaining butter. Cover and bake at 400° for 45 minutes. Remove the cover and return to oven to crisp for an additional 15 minutes. Remove chicken from pan and keep warm while making sauce.

Pour liquid from baking dish into a saucepan. Add flour and whisk into a paste. Add chicken broth and stir until thickened. Add wine and cream and stir over low heat until thick and smooth. Taste and adjust seasonings. Pour over chicken and serve.

Makes 8 servings

CREAMED CHICKEN FILLING

Use this fabulous filling for crepes, tortillas or puff pastry tarts.

1 bunch green onions, finely sliced
½ lb. mushrooms, sliced
½ cup butter
1½ lb. poached chicken breast meat, diced
½ cup cream sherry
2 cans (12 oz. each) evaporated milk
1¼ cups milk

½ cup flour
2½ tsp. salt
½ cup chopped cilantro
¾ cup sliced almonds, toasted
¾ cup diced green chiles
2 tbs. butter
¼ tsp. pepper
¼ tsp. cayenne pepper

In a skillet, sauté onions and mushrooms in butter until soft. Add chicken to sauté; set aside. In a heavy saucepan, combine sherry, evaporated milk, milk, flour and salt. Heat to a boil, stirring constantly until mixture thickens. Add cilantro and almonds. Add sautéed chicken mixture. In a separate skillet, sauté green chiles in 2 tbs. butter for 2 minutes and add to chicken mixture with pepper and cayenne. Taste and adjust seasonings.

Makes 1 quart

53

CREAMY CHICKEN WITH CHILE STRIPS

A popular Mexican dish, this goes well with rice, tortillas and a tossed salad loaded with crunchy vegetables.

6 chicken breast halves, boned and skinned
flour seasoned with salt and pepper
¼ cup butter
¼ cup vegetable oil
1 large onion
21 canned peeled green chiles
⅔ cup milk or half-and-half
½ tsp. salt
2 cups sour cream
⅓ lb. cheddar and/or Muenster cheese, grated

Cut each chicken breast half into 4 fillets. Dredge chicken fillets in seasoned flour. Heat butter and oil in a skillet and sauté chicken fillets until lightly browned; remove fillets to a plate and set aside. Cut onion into thin slices. Set aside 7 green chiles and cut remaining chiles into strips. Sauté onion, without browning, until soft. Add chile strips to onion and cook for an additional 5 minutes.

In a food processor or blender, blend 7 reserved chiles with milk until smooth. Add salt and sour cream and blend a few seconds longer. Arrange ½ of the chicken strips in a baking dish. Cover with ½ of the onion mixture, ½ of the chile sauce and ½ of the cheese. Repeat. Bake at 350° for 20 minutes or until cheese is melted completely.

Makes 6 servings

VELVET CHICKEN SOUP

This very delicate soup from China can also be used as a starter.

4 squares fresh bean curd, about 3-inch
4 oz. chicken breast meat, skinned
½ cup chicken broth
2 egg whites
salt to taste, if desired

½ tsp. white pepper
6 dried Chinese mushrooms
8 fresh spinach leaves
8 pieces barbecued pork
8 cups hot chicken broth
2 tbs. sesame oil

Drain bean curd and mash through a sieve. Mash chicken breast meat with flat side of cleaver and chop to a pulp (or use a food processor). Add ½ cup chicken broth a few drops at a time and blend until smooth. Beat egg whites slightly; mix with chicken pulp, mashed bean curd, salt and white pepper. Place mixture on an oiled plate and smooth. Soak mushroom in hot water, trim stem and cut into strips.

Place chicken mixture (on plate) in a steamer. Arrange mushrooms, spinach leaves and barbecued pork on top. Steam for 10 minutes, pour hot chicken broth on top and drizzle with sesame oil. Serve immediately.

Makes 8 servings

PICANTE CHICKEN FILLING

*Use this filling to stuff chile rellenos, enchiladas or
as a filling for tortillas for a quick meal.*

1 lb. chicken breast meat, skinned
2 tbs. vegetable oil
1 medium onion, diced
2 cloves garlic, minced
1/2 cup peeled, diced tomatoes
 (or more to taste)

1/2 cup raisins, plumped in hot
 water
1/2 cup slivered almonds, toasted
1 tsp. ground cumin
1/4 tsp. cinnamon
salt and pepper to taste

In a food processor or meat grinder, finely grind chicken meat. In a
skillet over medium heat, heat oil and sauté ground chicken meat, onion
and garlic until all pink in meat disappears. Add remaining ingredients
and cook 10 minutes longer. Taste and adjust seasonings.

Makes 4-5 cups

CHICKEN AND SOURDOUGH DUMPLINGS

Sourdough starter can be purchased at most grocery stores. It lends a unique flavor to an old-fashioned favorite.

6 tbs. melted butter
1/4 cup flour
1 1/2 cups chicken stock
1 can (13 oz.) evaporated milk
1 1/2 cups cream
1/2-1 tsp. salt

1/4 tsp. pepper, or to taste
1/2 cup chopped pimiento
2 1/2 lb. cooked chicken breast
  meat, skinned
Dumplings, follow

Melt butter in a saucepan, add flour and stir with a whisk until slightly browned. Add chicken stock and stir until slightly thickened. Turn heat down and add evaporated milk, cream, salt, pepper and pimiento. Taste and adjust seasonings. Cut chicken into bite-sized pieces. Add chicken to sauce and pour into a large casserole dish. Top with dumplings. Cook, uncovered, in a 350° oven for 10 to 15 minutes. Serve hot.

DUMPLINGS

2½ cups flour
½ tsp. salt
½ tsp. baking soda
1 tsp. baking powder
¾ cup milk

1 egg, beaten
½ cup sourdough starter
¼ cup melted butter
2 qt. boiling water

In a large mixing bowl, stir together flour, salt, baking soda and baking powder. In a sepatate bowl, combine milk, egg, sourdough starter and melted butter. Add to dry ingredients all at once, stirring until just moistened. Drop dough from a tablespoon into boiling water. (Dip spoon in hot liquid before dropping dumpling each time to help batter slide off easily.) Cover and simmer for 15 minutes. Remove with a slotted spoon and drain.

Makes 6-8 servings

FAST JAMBALAYA

*This easy-to-fix meal would go well with crusty
bread and a tossed salad or a fruit salad.*

4 slices bacon, diced
1 medium onion, chopped
½ small green bell pepper,
 chopped
2 cloves garlic, minced
1 cup canned tomatoes, with
 juice

1 tsp. tomato paste
1 cup diced poached chicken
12 precooked prawns
salt and pepper to taste
3 cups cooked rice

Place bacon in a skillet and cook until crisp. Remove bacon from skillet and drain off all but 1 tbs. bacon fat. Sauté onion, green pepper and garlic until vegetables are limp. Add remaining ingredients, including cooked bacon, and stir gently with a fork. Cover skillet, turn heat to low and let mixture cook until heated through.

Makes 6 servings

60

CREAMED CHICKEN ENCHILADAS

This very easy meal just takes minutes to fix. Serve it with a dollop of sour cream.

1 medium onion, chopped
2 tbs. butter
1 can (4 oz.) diced green chiles
1 can (14½ oz.) Spanish-style
  stewed tomatoes, drained
1 cup half-and-half

10 oz. cheddar cheese, grated
salt, pepper and ground cumin
  to taste
8 corn tortillas
1½ lb. poached chicken breast
  meat, shredded

In a skillet, sauté onion in butter until soft. Add green chiles, tomatoes, half-and-half and most of the cheese (reserve a little to sprinkle on top). Cook until cheese melts. Add seasonings to taste. Dip tortillas into sauce and spread out in a casserole dish. Fill tortillas with shredded chicken and roll. Arrange in casserole, seam side down. Cover rolled tortillas with remaining sauce and sprinkle with reserved cheese. Bake in a 350° oven for 30 minutes.

Makes 4 servings

CHICKEN AND PEPPER STIR-FRY

*The ingredients can be cut and prepared ahead of
time so that this dish can be quickly cooked
at the last minute. Serve with rice.*

1 lb. chicken breast meat, skinned
1 egg white, beaten
1/4 tsp. ground roasted Szechwan
  peppercorns
3/4 tsp. salt
3 tsp. sugar
1 tsp. dry sherry
2 1/2 tbs. soy sauce
2 red bell peppers
4 dried chili peppers, soaked in
  water

1/2-inch piece ginger root, peeled
6 cloves garlic, minced
1 tsp. cornstarch
black pepper to taste
2 tsp. vinegar
1 tbs. dry sherry
1 tsp. sesame oil
3 tbs. vegetable oil
1 cup cashews

Cut chicken into ¾-inch pieces and place in a bowl. Add egg white, ground peppercorns, ½ tsp. of the salt, 1 tsp. of the sugar, 1 tsp. sherry and 1 tbs. of the soy sauce. Mix and refrigerate for at least 30 minutes. Cut red pepper into ¾-inch chunks. Cut soaked chili peppers in half and remove seeds. Mince ginger root and mix with garlic. In a bowl, combine 2 tsp. sugar, cornstarch, ¼ tsp. salt, black pepper, 1½ tbs. soy sauce, vinegar, 1 tbs. sherry and sesame oil.

Heat oil in a wok or large skillet. Add cashews and toss until browned. Remove and drain on paper towels. (If desired, sprinkle with a little salt). Add chicken and stir-fry until chicken just turns white. Remove and set aside. Add red peppers, chili peppers, ginger and garlic and stir-fry for 30 seconds. Add chicken and remaining ingredients except cashews; stir-fry until mixture acquires a clear glaze. Add cashews and serve immediately.

Makes 4-6 servings

CHICKEN SAVOYARD

*This elegant French chicken entrée goes especially
well with asparagus.*

3 lb. chicken breast meat, skinned
salt, white pepper and nutmeg to taste
3 tbs. butter
1 tbs. flour
¼ cup dry white wine
¾ cup half-and-half
½ tsp. thyme
1 bay leaf
1 tsp. tarragon
2 cloves garlic, minced
1 egg yolk
1 tbs. lemon juice
½ cup shredded Swiss or Muenster cheese
½ cup soft breadcrumbs
1 tbs. chopped parsley

Cut chicken into long strips and sprinkle with salt, white pepper and nutmeg. In a skillet, heat 2 tbs. of the butter and brown chicken strips. Remove chicken and place in a shallow baking dish in a single layer. Stir flour into skillet; add wine and half-and-half, stirring to loosen browned particles on bottom of skillet. Stir until sauce thickens slightly. Add thyme, bay leaf, tarragon and garlic. Beat egg yolk with lemon juice. Add a little hot mixture to egg yolk and stir; add egg mixture to skillet, stirring to combine. Add cheese and cook over low heat until cheese melts. Pour sauce over chicken in baking dish.

Melt remaining 1 tbs. butter. Mix breadcrumbs with parsley and butter. Sprinkle buttered breadcrumbs over chicken. Bake in a 375° oven for 35 minutes or until chicken is done and topping is well browned. Remove bay leaf and serve immediately.

Makes 6 servings

STUFFED CHICKEN BREASTS SUPREME

Chicken breasts are filled with a delicious ham and cheese stuffing and smothered in a creamy Parmesan sauce.

6 whole chicken breasts, boned and skinned
2 tbs. brandy

STUFFING

1/4 cup butter
2 tbs. chopped shallots
1 tsp. minced garlic
1/2 lb. smoked ham, ground

1/2 tsp. dried thyme
1/2 cup fresh breadcrumbs
1/2 cup grated Gruyère cheese
2 tbs. chopped parsley

SAUCE

1/4 cup butter
1/4 cup brandy
2 tbs. butter
1 tsp. garlic
2 tbs. chopped shallots
3 tbs. flour
2 tsp. tarragon

1 cup dry white wine
1/2 cup chicken broth
1/2 cup cream
2 tbs. chopped mushrooms
salt and white pepper to taste
2 tbs. grated Parmesan cheese

Cut a pocket in the thick side of each chicken breast. Brush pockets with 2 tbs. brandy and set aside.

To make stuffing: In a skillet, heat butter and cook shallots and garlic over medium heat for 3 minutes. Remove from heat and stir in ham, thyme, breadcrumbs, Gruyère cheese and parsley, mixing well. Place 1 tbs. stuffing in each breast pocket. Pinch to seal.

To make sauce: In a skillet, heat ¼ cup butter and sauté chicken over high heat, just to stiffen, not to brown. Remove chicken from skillet. Pour brandy into skillet and stir to loosen browned particles. Add 2 tbs. butter, garlic and shallots and cook for 1 minute. Stir in flour and cook for 2 minutes. Add tarragon, wine, chicken broth, cream and mushrooms. Cook and stir over medium heat until sauce thickens. Season with salt and white pepper and add Parmesan. Taste and adjust seasonings. Return chicken to skillet, baste with sauce, cover and simmer for 15 minutes or until chicken feels firm to the touch. Do not overcook.

Makes 6 large servings

CHICKEN RAVIOLI

*A tender chicken and rosemary filling makes a
tempting ravioli that is good with just a sprinkling of grated
Romano cheese or a light cream sauce.*

DOUGH

4 eggs
3 cups flour

1 tbs. vegetable oil
1 tsp. salt

Mix ingredients together and knead until smooth. Allow dough to rest, covered, until filling is made.

FILLING

1½ lb. cooked chicken breast
  meat
2 tbs. butter
½ cup chopped onion

½ tsp. ground rosemary
salt and pepper to taste
1 egg white, beaten for sealing
  dough

In a food processor or meat grinder, coarsely grind chicken. Melt butter in a skillet and sauté onion until soft. Add chicken, rosemary, salt and pepper. Taste and adjust seasonings.

To make ravioli: Break dough into 4 pieces, covering unused dough. Roll dough as thin as possible into strips, or cut into 3-inch circles. Place 1 tsp. filling every 2 inches across and down in a checker-board fashion or fill each round. Dip finger in egg white and make vertical and horizontal lines between teaspoons of filling or around edges of circle. Cover with second sheet (or rounds) of pasta and press down firmly along egg white lines. Cut strips into squares with a pastry wheel. Let dry for at least ½ hour before cooking.

To cook ravioli: Drop in rapidly boiling salted water and stir very gently. Boil for 6 to 8 minutes or until tender. Drain carefully in a large colander.

Makes 36

CHICKEN BREAST SCALOPPINE

Make this quick dish more elegant with shredded prosciutto.

4 chicken breast halves, boned
  and skinned
flour seasoned with salt and
  pepper
6 tbs. butter
3 tbs. olive oil

¾ lb. mushrooms, sliced
salt and pepper to taste
½ cup dry Marsala wine
2 tbs. finely minced parsley
shredded prosciutto ham for
  garnish, optional

Place chicken breasts between waxed paper sheets and pound until double original size. Dredge chicken in seasoned flour. Melt 3 tbs. of the butter and all of the oil in a skillet and cook chicken over medium heat until lightly browned on both sides. Transfer pieces to a serving platter and keep warm. Melt remaining butter in skillet and sauté mushrooms over medium high heat. Season with salt and pepper. When mushrooms are lightly browned, add wine and parsley; boil for 2 minutes. Pour over chicken and serve immediately. If desired, garnish with prosciutto strips.

Makes 4 servings

BREAKFAST CROISSANT

Make an elegant breakfast on a split croissant, topped with poached eggs, chicken and bacon and smothered in a delicious cream sauce.

3 tbs. butter
3 tbs. flour
2 cups milk
3 oz. cream cheese
salt and white pepper to taste
4 croissants

2 whole poached chicken
  breasts, boned and skinned
8 slices bacon, fried and drained
8 poached eggs
grated cheddar cheese for garnish

In a saucepan, melt butter and stir in flour. Cook for 1 minute on medium heat, add milk and stir until thickened. Add cream cheese, salt and pepper and stir until cheese melts. Taste and adjust seasonings.

To serve: Split each croissant (if desired, toast lightly to make a flakier pastry), and place on a serving plate. Cut chicken into thin strips, lay over croissant halves, place 1 slice bacon on each half and top with a poached egg. Cover with sauce and sprinkle with cheese. Broil until heated and cheese melts. Serve immediately.

Makes 4 servings

ORIENTAL CHICKEN CUBES

*This is a special frying technique that creates a
crispy outside coating and leaves the inside tender and succulent.
Serve with rice and stir-fried vegetables.*

1½ lb. chicken breast meat, skinned
½ tbs. soy sauce
½ tsp. salt
pinch white pepper
oil for deep frying
1 tbs. vegetable oil
2-3 cloves garlic, minced
2 green onions, diced
1 tbs. soy sauce
2 tbs. dry sherry
½ tsp. sugar

Cut chicken meat into 1½-inch cubes and place in a bowl with soy sauce, salt and white pepper. Stir to coat. Let stand for 1 hour to marinate. Heat frying oil to 350°. Drain chicken and fry for 3 minutes. Remove chicken cubes with a strainer and increase heat to 375°. Return chicken to pan and fry for an additional 2 to 3 minutes or until golden brown. Drain.

In a skillet, heat 1 tbs. oil and add garlic and green onions, stirring quickly. Do not let garlic brown (this tends to make garlic bitter). Add soy sauce, sherry and sugar and mix to combine. Stir in chicken until all pieces are coated and serve immediately.

Makes 4 servings

QUICK GOLDEN CHICKEN

The golden color comes from turmeric, which is very good for you.

4 whole chicken breasts, boned
½ cup vegetable oil
2 tsp. salt
4 tsp. turmeric
⅔ cup sour cream, cream or
  coconut cream

1 tsp. ground cardamom
1 tsp. ground cumin
6 tbs. mango chutney
enough milk to thin consistency,
  optional

If desired, remove chicken skin. Pound meat slightly to a consistent thickness for even grilling. In a bowl, mix oil, salt and turmeric together. Brush on chicken and grill or barbecue until cooked through, about 5 to 7 minutes per side. In a saucepan, mix together cream, cardamom, cumin and chutney. Add enough milk to make a medium thick sauce. Place over medium low heat until just heated through. Serve with grilled chicken or drizzled down the center of the serving platter under chicken.

Makes 8 servings

CHICKEN WITH MUSTARD SAUCE

Here's a quick sauté that just takes minutes to fix.

2 whole chicken breasts, skinned
3 tbs. vegetable oil
2 shallots, minced (or ¼ cup chopped onion)
2 cloves garlic, minced
1 tbs. Dijon mustard

2 tbs. grainy Dijon mustard
¼ cup dry white wine
1 cup half-and-half
salt and white pepper to taste
chopped parsley or chives for garnish

Split chicken breasts into halves. Heat 2 tbs. of the oil in a skillet and quickly sauté breasts until brown on both sides and almost cooked through. Remove from skillet and keep warm while making sauce. Add shallots to skillet and cook for 2 minutes. Add garlic and cook until wilted but not brown. Remove skillet from heat. Stir in both mustards, add wine and return to heat. Stir to loosen particles on bottom of skillet. Cook for 5 minutes, add half-and-half and reduce heat. Cook over low heat until sauce thickens. Add salt and white pepper. Return chicken to skillet and heat. Sprinkle with chopped parsley and serve immediately.

Makes 4 servings

INDEX